Flower Gardening:
PERENNIALS
The Gardener's Collection

Better Homes and Gardens® Books
Des Moines

MEREDITH® BOOKS
President, Book Group: Joseph J. Ward
Vice President and Editorial Director: Elizabeth P. Rice
Art Director: Ernest Shelton

PERENNIALS
Senior Editor: Marsha Jahns
Editor: Cathy Howard
Art Director: Michael Burns
Designer: John Howard
Copy Editors: Durrae Johanek, David Walsh
Assistant Editor: Jennifer Weir
Administrative Assistant: Carla Horner
Special thanks: Thomas E. Eltzroth

MEREDITH CORPORATION CORPORATE OFFICERS:
Chairman of the Executive Committee: E. T. Meredith III
**Chairman of the Board, President
   and Chief Executive Officer:** Jack D. Rehm
Group Presidents:
   Joseph J. Ward, Books
   William T. Kerr, Magazines
   Philip A. Jones, Broadcasting
   Allen L. Sabbag, Real Estate
Vice Presidents:
   Leo R. Armatis, Corporate Relations
   Thomas G. Fisher, General Counsel and Secretary
   Larry D. Hartsook, Finance
   Michael A. Sell, Treasurer
   Kathleen J. Zehr, Controller and Assistant Secretary

*All of us at Meredith® Books are dedicated to providing you
with the information and ideas you need to garden success-
fully. We guarantee your satisfaction with this book for as
long as you own it. If you have any questions, comments, or
suggestions, please write to us at:*

MEREDITH® BOOKS, Garden Books
Editorial Department, RW 240
1716 Locust St.,
Des Moines, IA 50309-3023

Perennials are like faithful friends: trustworthy, reliable, and there when you need them. You can count on them to come early, stay late, and be there in between, when nothing else is in bloom. Planted as the backbone of a mixed flower border, perennials promise to return year after year, providing a pleasing variety of colors, textures, shapes, and heights.

CONTENTS

Using Perennials 6

Planning Your Perennial Garden 20

Growing Beautiful Perennials 28

Directory of Perennials 42

Zone Map 62

Index 64

Using Perennials

*L*ook at any well-planned flower garden and you're almost certain to see plenty of perennials. And with good reason. Year after year, perennials offer an ever-changing framework of color and texture, filling gardens with spectacular flowers and foliage.

Perennials in the Landscape

Starting with Perennials
Perennials should be the main ingredient in any garden. In addition to filling a garden with beautiful flowers and foliage, they don't require the time and expense of yearly replanting, unlike annuals. Most will grow and bloom for many years without a lot of pampering. This sense of permanence adds continuity to a garden.

Selection Process With so many colors, shapes, and textures available, it often is difficult to decide which perennials to include in a garden. To get ideas, look through gardening books and magazines, visit garden centers and public or private gardens, and order garden catalogs from nurseries that specialize in perennials.

Many gardeners eventually find a particular plant they like and collect as many varieties of it as they can find. Daylilies, hostas, lilies, dahlias, geraniums, lavender, and iris are a few popular types.

Investments and Dividends A perennial garden need not be an expensive investment, unless you want to plant an entire garden in a single season. Take your cue from other gardeners. Most build their collections of perennials slowly over the years, investing a few dollars each year. Trading plants with fellow gardeners is another good way to expand your collection and save money, as well.

Whatever your initial investment in perennials, however, consider it money well spent. Look at the perennials as an investment in your property and your personal pleasure. You'll receive years of enjoyment for just pennies a year.

Arches offer a permanent backdrop for this beautiful garden filled with old-fashioned perennials.

Perennials in the Landscape

Versatility Plus For sheer versatility, it's hard to imagine a more valuable type of plant than perennials. Whether your goal is to re-create Grandmother's cottage garden or to develop a dramatic English border, to spice up a sunny path or to color a cool, shady bower, look to perennials.

Their wide array of heights, colors, shapes, and foliage is multiplied by their seasonal span. And where some perennials demand hot, dry soil, others clamor for shade and moist conditions. Because of their diversity, you can find perennials suited to nearly every garden setting and condition.

Gardener's Tip

For containers, annuals are the choice of many gardeners. But perennials will perform prettily in pots, too.

Myriad Uses Mass perennials for brilliant displays of color, or use them as edgings along borders or paths. Plant aster, delphinium, iris, daisy, baby's-breath, peony, and dianthus for cut flowers. Grow lavender, phlox, and feverfew for their heady fragrances.

Use perennials to take advantage of overlooked nooks and crannies. Or transform the thin strips of soil on either side of a path or walk into a festival of flowers.

Sun-loving varieties that tolerate drought, such as sedum, spurge, and santolina, are ideal in a rock garden setting. Shade-loving plants like hostas, astilbe, primrose, bleeding-heart, columbine, and Japanese anemone will brighten a garden without sunshine.

Pair perennials with contrasting foliage, such as the swordlike stalks of bearded iris and the lacy leaves of columbine, to extend the show after their fleeting blooms fade.

Perennials for Special Conditions

Because of their diversity, you can find perennials suited to nearly every garden situation. Use cranesbill geranium or daylily in poor soil with little organic matter.

Where soil is moist or boggy, pick plants such as astilbe. Oriental poppy and yarrow tolerate dry soils. Try hostas or ferns for areas with half-day shade or dappled shade all day.

Most plants listed under poor soil grow better in well-prepared and properly fertilized soils. Those listed under dry soil also grow well in moister conditions, especially if given good drainage.

Poor Soil Where soil is poor, plant aloe, baby's-breath, candytuft, catnip, cerastium, daylily, geranium (cranesbill), globe thistle, hardy ageratum, leadwort, moss phlox, oenothera, rudbeckia, sedum, stachys, swamp saxifrage, thyme, verbascum, Virginia bluebells, and yarrow.

Wet Soil Where soil is wet, plant astilbe, bee balm, bergenia, blue flag, eupatorium, ferns, forget-me-not, galax, globeflower, helenium, Japanese iris, lobelia, loosestrife, lungwort, marsh marigold, spiderwort, swamp milkweed, swamp saxifrage, sweet woodruff, violet, and yellow flag.

Dry Soil Where soil is dry, plant aloe, anthemis, baby's-breath, baptisia, butterfly weed, coreopsis, gaillardia, helianthus, leadwort, Oriental poppy, poker plant, rudbeckia, santolina, sedum, spurge, sweet william, thrift, yarrow, and yucca.

Daylilies are a good choice for gardens with poor soil.

Perennials for Special Conditions

Shade-Tolerant Perennials Shady conditions present one of the more vexing problems for gardeners who want a lot of colorful blossoms. Fortunately, perennials offer many choices for areas with full or dappled shade.

The following plants offer lovely foliage, flowers, or both under low-light conditions: astilbe, balloon flower, bee balm, bleeding-heart, columbine, coralbells, ferns, forget-me-not, galax, gas plant, globeflower, helleborus, hosta, hypericum, Jacob's-ladder, Japanese anemone, lily-of-the-valley, lobelia, loosestrife, Maltese-cross, penstemon, physostegia, primrose, spiderwort, swamp rose mallow, thalictrum, and Virginia bluebells.

Beautifully Foliaged Perennials Lacy leaves, glossy texture, or variegated greenery can have as much dramatic impact as a colorful blossom in the overall effect of the garden tapestry. Foliage color, form, and texture are key elements of your design.

Perennials that offer lovely foliage along with their flowers include: astilbe, baneberry (*Actaea sp.*), bellwort (*Uvularia sp.*), bleeding-heart, bloodroot (*Sanguinaria sp.*), burnet (*Sanguisorba sp.*), gas plant, goutweed or bishop's-weed (*Aegopodium podagraria*), hosta, iris, lily-of-the-valley, moss phlox, mountain spurge, peony, perennial pea (*Lathyrus sp.*), Solomon's-seal (*Polygonatum sp.*), stachys, and violet.

Long-Lived Perennials Many perennials are exceptionally long livers. Their ranks include astilbe, balloon flower, baptista, bleeding-heart, campanula, daylily, gas plant, hardy aster, hosta, iris, monkshood, peony, phlox, veronica, and yucca.

Hostas, astilbe, and low-growing evergreens add color and texture to this shady perennials border.

Seasons of Color

Careful planning will reward you with a mixed perennial border that is abloom from spring to frost. Because most perennials blossom for just a few weeks, you'll need to plant a variety of perennials, biennials, and annuals that bloom at successive intervals.

Interplanting is a big reason for the success of the garden shown here. Perennials are generously distributed throughout, with blocks of annuals and biennials planted between them.

Seasonal Color For color early in the growing season, take your cue from this spring garden (above right), where blue forget-me-nots, English daisies, Iceland poppies, felicia, and coralbells splash their vibrant color. Follow them with plants that bloom later, when the spring colors start to fade. In the summer garden (opposite), perennial sedum, rudbeckias, and campanulas team up with annuals (petunias, marigolds, and zinnias) for a brilliant show.

Changing Focus This constant flow of changing color will shift the garden's focal points of attention as the seasons change, yielding a garden alive with color.

With experience and study, the strategy of having color during each season comes naturally. When the foliage of spring bulbs fades, fill in with young annual plants. Then replant areas once filled with cool-season bedding plants, using tender bulbs and more annuals for warm weather.

Seasons of Color

Season of bloom is as important as plant height when you plan your perennial garden. For best show, choose plants from each of the three major blooming seasons for all height categories. Use the following lists to achieve steady color as the seasons progress.

Spring (February to May): adonis, ajuga, anchusa, *Anemone canadensis,* artemisia Silver Mound, basket-of-gold alyssum, bleeding-heart, buttercup, candytuft, crocus (bulb), dianthus (*Dianthus x allwoodi), doronicum, dwarf iris, geum, grape hepatica, *Phlox subulata*, poppy (*Papaver burseri*), and viola.

Summer (May to August): anchusa, anthemis, astilbe, baby's-breath, balloon flower, bellflower, bee balm, butterfly weed, columbine, coreopsis, coralbells, daylily, delphinium, gaillardia, gas plant, globe thistle, helenium, heliopsis, iris, lamb's-ears, liatris, lobelia, loosestrife, peony, phlox, poppy, rudbeckia, salvia (*Salvia azurea*), shasta daisy, spiderwort (*Tradescantia sp.*), thermopsis, thrift, veronica, and yarrow.

Fall (August to Frost): *anemone hupehensis,* candytuft ('Autumn Snow' variety), chrysanthemum, daylilies (late-season varieties), hardy aster, *Helleborus niger* (Christmas rose), hosta (*Hosta tardiflora*), sedum, and spiderwort (*Tradescantia* variety 'Blue Stone').

The crowning glory of a fall garden, chrysanthemums (above) come in all sizes of flowers and in every color but blue.

Veronica, coreopsis, balloon flower, phlox, monarda, and lythrum make a harmonious ensemble (opposite).

Planning Your Perennial Garden

A prizewinning perennial garden is one that gets its natural look from careful planning on the part of the gardener. When perennials are combined attractively in an informal design, each one gets a turn to star in an ongoing floral show.

Planning and Design

Proper Planning Most perennial gardeners strive for a succession of blooms during spring, summer, and fall. That means juggling bloom times and heights of several perennial varieties. Their changing colors, sizes, and textures make landscaping a complex art form.

Consider color, soil, sun and shade conditions, planting, care, growth habits, and foliage of some of your favorite perennials as you plan your garden. Don't let fear of failure keep you from trying. Relocating plants is one of the rites of spring!

Choosing Colors Color can be the framework of your garden design, providing accent, balance, repetition, and excitement. When combining perennials, choose a color scheme for each season, using one main color as the backbone. Make yellow the focus for spring, pink for early summer, blue for midsummer, and gold for fall, for example.

Choose blues and violets, which are cooler colors, to make your

garden appear larger. Bolder reds, oranges, and yellows add warmth.

Select a few plants in each chosen color range, then sprinkle in a few secondary perennials in complementary colors. Use brightly foliaged plants in your scheme, too.

To avoid a checkerboard effect with small isolated spots of color, plant each perennial en masse and repeat throughout the border. For contrast, put similar or opposite colors near the massed colors.

Although these perennial gardens (above and opposite) look informal, they are carefully planned.

Planning and Design

Shapes and Textures Variety in form and foliage adds spice to a garden. Use a mixture of mat and cushion plants, medium and large mounded plants, and plants with spiked blossoms. Types of foliage plants include coarse and soft, lance shape and rounded, and flat and glossy. Be sure to use a variety of plant heights to add tension and drama to your garden design.

Varying shapes and textures (above and opposite) give a garden appeal.

Garden Style Formal or informal? It all depends on your taste and the style of your home. Formal gardens are symmetrical; the more popular informal gardens are amorphous and most effective when laid out in curving drifts.

Sun or Shade First consider the amount of sun your garden receives during most of the season. If it gets direct sun only a couple of hours each day, or gets dappled shade most of the day, use plants suited to shade. Areas receiving at least six hours of direct sun every day are suitable for full-sun perennials.

Borders Make your border at least 4 to 6 feet deep, and plant perennials so they're tapered in height. If the border is backed by a wall or fence, plant tall varieties in back and low growers in front. To enjoy an island bed from all sides, plant taller perennials in the center, shorter ones on the edges. Group three or more of one variety in drifts for visual impact.

As a rule, plan areas of plants rather than rows or single plants scattered throughout your garden. Group together three to five plants of a variety. Plant them in the shape of a triangle or in no particular shape at all.

Selecting Perennials by Height

Successful borders such as the two shown here have plantings that are staggered in height from the low growers at the front (right) to the tallest varieties at the back (opposite). To achieve this informal tapering from front to back without abrupt changes in height, make borders at least 4 to 6 feet deep. The deeper the bed, the more gracefully you can arrange an ascending order of plants.

For deep borders, you can put a few stepping-stones throughout the plantings so you can weed and

tend to the plants' needs without walking through the bed and destroying the soil texture.

Gardener's Tip

Why not photograph your garden? To help you remember where you've planted flowers, take photographs throughout the seasons. That way you'll also have records you can use for future landscape changes.

Front of Border (Dwarf to 15 Inches): anemone (*A. canadensis*), creeping baby's-breath, bellflower, brunnera, candytuft, chrysanthemum (cushion varieties), cranesbill geranium, crocus, dianthus, dwarf iris varieties, English daisy, feverfew, flax, hardy aster (dwarf michaelmas varieties), lavender, leadwort (dwarf), painted daisy, phlox (*P. subulata*), potentilla, primrose, salvia (*S. azurea*), 'Silver Mound' artemisia, stokesia, veronica (some varieties), and viola.

Mid-Border (15 to 30 Inches):
astilbe, balloon flower, bee balm, bleeding-heart, butterfly weed, chrysanthemum (many varieties), columbine, coralbells, coreopsis, delphinium, foxglove, gaillardia, gas plant, hosta (*H. lancifolia* types), lilies, lobelia, loosestrife, peony, phlox, poppy, rudebeckia, shasta daisy, spiderwort (*Tradescantia sp.*), and Virginia bluebells.

Back of Border (Over 30 Inches):
anchusa ('Dropmore' variety), baby's-breath (*Gypsophila paniculata*), baptisia, daylily,

delphinium (species varieties), foxglove (some varieties), globe thistle, hardy aster, helenium, helianthus, heliopsis, hibiscus, hollyhock, hosta, liatris, lilies (many hybrid varieties), lupine, phlox (*P. paniculata*), rudbeckia, solidago, thermopsis, verbascum, yarrow ('Coronation Gold' variety), and yucca.

Growing Beautiful Perennials

Perennials perform well with average care, but will reward you with bountiful blooms if given a little extra attention. Here's how to give them a push toward perfection.

Planting Basics

Preparing the Soil A perennial grows in the same spot for many years. Preparing soil in the bed is the first step toward getting a plant of top-notch quality, such as those shown here (right and opposite).

As early in spring as you can work the ground, turn the soil the full depth of the spade. Work the topsoil toward the bottom; this is where the perennials' roots will get most of their nourishment. Rake the ground level, and cover with 2 to 4 inches of organic matter such as well-rotted cow manure, compost, peat moss, or a combination. Blend it into the soil with a garden spade or spading fork.

It's almost impossible to add too much organic matter. This material lightens heavy clay soil, improves the tilth of good soil, and increases the water- and nutrient-holding capacity of sandy soils, so don't be afraid to add large quantities. A compost heap is the least expensive source of organic matter; start one if you haven't already, and keep it going in your garden.

Planting Although planting tips vary somewhat with each perennial, these steps will help ensure success for most.

■ Set newly purchased or divided plants at the proper depth: the same level they grew the previous season. You'll be able to see marks of the original depth on the dormant stems.

■ Next, provide adequate space for roots so they're not crowded. Dig a hole several inches larger in

Planting Basics

diameter than the spread of the roots, and space the roots in all directions so they get established quickly. Hint: Build a cone of earth at the bottom of the hole, then stretch the roots out over it.

■ Gradually sprinkle in soil.

■ Water well and add more soil to bring the level even with the surrounding ground. Your main goal in transplanting—whether you have a new plant or one obtained through division of an older plant—is to avoid shocking the plant excessively. Don't let roots dry out or break off; they're the plant's lifeline to food, moisture, and good health.

■ Provide plenty of breathing room between perennials. Air circulation reduces risk of mold and mildew. Proper spacing also eliminates excessive competition for soil moisture and nutrients so your plants can grow to full size.

Labeling On short stakes, label the locations of newly planted perennials, especially if planting in fall. Some plants are late to emerge in spring, and it is easy to forget their locations or which plant is which. Because labels can be lost, keep a permanent record of plants as well. Record locations of all plants, the year and month they were planted, and where they were obtained. This information can come in handy later on.

Staking Tall-growing perennials, such as delphinium, lupine, and foxglove, need to be staked. Don't wait until the plants have toppled to give them support. Put the stakes in early, and keep plants tied or trained to stakes or wire-frame supports. If transplanting tall plants in mid-season when they have large, heavy leaves, tie the foliage to a stake to keep leaves off the ground and to steady the plant while the roots take hold.

Perennials are healthier when given a little breathing space.

Care and Maintenance

Dividing Perennials Perennials benefit from being divided every few years. Fresh soil for their roots and a new start result in a stronger, better-blooming plant. Even if you don't want more plants, divide old clumps occasionally.

Some perennials can be separated by cutting or gently pulling off sections of the crown. Use a hand fork or a sharp knife for tuberous or woody roots. Don't make too many divisions from one plant. Be sure each has enough roots to sustain growth.

■ Wash all or most of the soil away from the roots so you can see where you're cutting. Direct a stream of water into the root area to get the soil out.

■ Keep as many roots attached to each division as possible, but trim away any damaged roots. If any part looks dead or diseased, trim all the way back to clean, white tissue.

Feeding and Watering The first year is the most critical for any perennial.

■ Watch foliage for signs of wilting and damage caused by insects or disease.

■ Keep the soil moist, but don't overwater.

■ Avoid, also, the temptation to overfeed. Your plants will be much stronger if they are fed just enough to make normal yearly growth. If fertilized too much, growth will be rank, weak, and plants will be less able to withstand winter damage.

■ In early spring, apply an all-purpose fertilizer, such as 5-10-5, and water in lightly. For an extra boost during the blooming season, apply water-soluble plant food to the foliage and soil.

Mulching After the soil has warmed up in spring, apply a light summer mulch of organic material to keep weeds down.

Perennials like these hardy asters will bloom more vigorously if they're divided every few years.

Care and Maintenance

■ In the fall, apply a winter mulch thickly to cover the perennial beds. It can be wood chips, straw, peat moss, bark, shredded bark, or decaying leaves.

Weeding It's an onerous chore, but somebody's got to do it. If you're the designated weeder, remember that the best offense against weeds is a good defense.

■ When preparing your beds in the fall for spring planting, nip weeds in the bud by covering the beds with several thicknesses of mulch. This will eventually decay. In the meantime, it forms a weed barrier and in the spring you can poke holes through it to plant your perennials.

■ Weed regularly, particularly in the spring when growth is aggressive. Avoid herbicides.

Pinching Back "A pinch to grow on" is a good policy for some perennials. In particular, many types of chrysanthemums

(opposite) and asters need pinching to encourage branching. This is especially true of varieties that grow on long stems, such as decorative mums.

■ Pinching should begin when the plants are about 6 inches tall in the spring. Pinch back about 2 inches. When a new top grows and more branches develop, pinch them all back again about 2 inches. Repeat in midsummer, and then allow flower buds to develop. This helps plants produce strong stems and abundant blossoms.

Propagating Perennials

You can beat the price of buying plants by starting many of your perennials from seeds, cuttings, or root divisions. Increasing your supply of perennials usually is a simple operation, once you know the process for each type of plant. Some perennials must be started from root cuttings, some come readily from seed, many will propagate from stem cuttings, and others are increased by division of the plant's crown.

Root Cuttings Take root cuttings when the plant is in active growth, usually in the spring. Lift the plant, wash soil from the roots, and cut the fleshiest roots into three-inch sections; plant these horizontally with a half-inch cover of soil. Replant the parent plant.

Seeds You can produce many more perennials from seeds with much less expense than buying them already grown. The disadvantages are the time required before they bloom (sometimes months) and unpredictable flower colors.

■ Plant perennial seeds in either spring or late summer (in sufficient time so the young plants are sturdy enough to make it through the first winter). Plant and care for the seedlings as you do annual seedlings by keeping them watered and lightly fed.

■ Many mail-order catalogs offer perennial seeds. You can collect seeds from your garden if you leave a few faded flowers to form seedpods. Pick seeds when the pods are dried and brown. Spread a few around the base of plants, and some may start on their own in the spring.

Stem cuttings quickly result in healthy young plants. Take 2- to 3-inch cuttings, and strip off all but a few leaves at the tip. Insert the stem end an inch or so into a bed of moist vermiculite, and cover with a plastic sheet. Set the flat

Start baby's-breath from seeds sown directly in the garden in spring.

Propagating Perennials

where it gets bright light but no direct sun. In two weeks, the cuttings will probably be well rooted and ready to be set in your perennial border.

Dividing the crown of a plant is sometimes a big job but results in several good-size plants. Lift the plant and wash soil from the roots. With some plants, you can pull sections of the crown free, but most require a sharp knife for cutting through the fleshy crown.

Room to Grow If you have space, start a nursery to keep all your young plants in one spot until they are big enough to set out in the garden. Feed lightly the first year so you get firm, sturdy growth. A cold frame is valuable for most plants. It is especially helpful for starting perennials from seed and for overwintering young plants from cuttings or plants that are only marginally hardy.

Winter Protection After the first killing frost—usually preceded by several light frosts that nip the tops

of plants but do not kill the foliage back to the ground—it's time to prepare perennials for winter.

First, cut and remove dead stalks, trimming stems to within 4 inches of the ground. Once you've cleared the beds of dead foliage and weeds, apply a winter mulch of straw or peat moss, using sections of chicken wire or branches to hold it down.

Oriental poppies (above) like cold winters.

Prepare perennials for winter to help ensure beautiful spring and summer blooms (opposite).

Directory of Perennials

Before you plant perennials, study their needs and characteristics. Read this section for information on season of bloom; zonal hardiness; height of plant at maturity; preferences for sun, shade, or soil type; color or colors available; and special cultural information about some of the more popular species.

Directory of Perennials

ADONIS
Also called spring adonis
Adonis vernalis

Zone: 3

Height: 12 inches

Bloom Time: March to April

Comments: An early bloomer, adonis is often the first plant in the perennial garden to show color. Its feathery green foliage and bright yellow blossoms are a welcome sight after a long, colorless winter.

The plant grows well in sunny locations and tolerates most soil types, but for best results, the plants need a constant supply of moisture. Use adonis in rock gardens and along the front of the border where its early color can be appreciated. It also works well in a mass or mixed with wildflowers. Propagate from seeds sown during spring and fall. Divide mature plants in late spring or fall.

AGERATUM, HARDY
Also called mist flower
Eupatorium coelestinum

Zone: 3

Height: 2 to 3 feet

Bloom Time: August to September

Comments: Hardy ageratum is valuable for late-summer color in a perennial border. Its many flowers are bright blue. The plant requires little attention and does best in a slightly shaded location. Plants grow in clumps and are extra showy in mass plantings. To propagate, take root cuttings in early spring.

ALYSSUM
Also called basket-of-gold alyssum
Aurinia saxatilis

Zone: 3

Height: 8 to 15 inches

Bloom Time: Spring

Comments: Often confused with the annual flower sweet alyssum, basket-of-gold alyssum is grown primarily for its brilliant golden blossoms set against soft-textured gray foliage. The plant is low growing, making it a good choice for rock gardens, on slopes, as edgings, or combined with spring-flowering bulbs. Plant in full sun or partial shade in well-drained soil. Shear plants to half their height after flowering.

Start plants from seeds sown outdoors in late summer or spring or take stem cuttings anytime in summer. In cold climates, overwinter young plants in a cold frame or a sheltered location. Divide every three years to renew old plants.

ARTEMISIA
Also called wormwood
Artemisia sp.

Zone: 3

Height: Varies with variety

Bloom Time: Spring through summer

Comments: Wormwoods are grown for their attractive, fine-textured gray-green foliage, rather than for their flowers. Many have a

delicate scent of lemon or camphor. They are attractive set against dark-foliaged plants, and provide a soft visual barrier between plants with sharply contrasting flower colors. Their foliage color blends especially well with pinks and blues.

Plant in full sun in any type of well-drained soil. Propagate by dividing in spring or by taking stem cuttings during early summer. Keep stem cuttings slightly dry to prevent rot.

ASTER, HARDY
Also called michaelmas daisy
Aster sp.

Zone: 4

Height: 3 to 4 feet

Bloom Time: Late summer to fall

Comments: Asters are a sure bet if you want reliable color in late summer and fall. They require full sun and thrive in moist, well-drained, fertilized soil. Provide support for tall types. Remove faded flowers to keep plants tidy and prevent self-sowing.

Divide plants in spring or fall. Replant only the most vigorous divisions from around the outside of the clump. Except in mild climates, division every three or four years is sufficient.

ASTILBE
Also called false spirea
Astilbe x arendsi

Zone: 4

Height: 15 to 30 inches

Bloom Time: Early summer

Comments: Astilbes are ideal for areas of partial shade or full morning sun and afternoon shade. During late spring and early summer, they produce fluffy flower spikes in white, cream, and shades of pink, salmon, and red atop glossy fernlike mounds of foliage. Water regularly, especially during hot, dry spells, and fertilize at least once just after flowering. Avoid cultivation, which damages the shallow roots. Divide in spring just before the start of new growth.

Astilbe

BABY'S-BREATH
Gypsophila paniculata

Zone: 3

Height: To 4 feet

Bloom Time: Early summer

Comments: Few plants can equal the cloudlike display of a group of baby's-breath, with their dainty masses of white or light pink flowers held above small foliage on wiry stems. Flowering is heaviest in early to midsummer but continues lightly for the rest of the season if you cut the flowers before they go to seed. Flowers are widely used in fresh arrangements and corsages, and they dry well.

Plant in full sun, in well-drained, but not too fertile, soil. Because baby's-breath doesn't transplant well, start from seeds sown directly in the garden in spring; or use compressed peat moss pots and sow a small group of seeds in each. Thin all but the strongest seedlings. Or use stem cuttings taken in midsummer.

BEE BALM
Also called bergamot
Monarda didyma

Zone: 4

Height: 2 to 3 feet

Bloom Time: Summer to early fall

Comments: Quick growing and attractive, bee balm is ideal for mid- to back-of-the-border locations. Tall stalks bear clusters of flowers, usually red, but also white, pink, and lavender. Bee balm attracts bees and butterflies.

An aromatic herb in the mint family, bee balm grows best in slightly shaded spot in moist, rich soil. Don't plant bee balm where it might crowd nearby weaker plants. It's good for naturalizing in woodland and bog gardens. or root Propagate by dividing in spring, or root newly cut stem cuttings in late spring.

BLEEDING-HEART
Dicentra spectabilis

Zone: 4

Height: 1½ to 2 feet

Bloom Time: Spring

Comments: Every year, reliable and long-favored bleeding-heart brightens the spring garden with its gracefully arching stems of pink to rose heart-shape flowers.

Plant in a partially shaded location in moist soil enriched with organic matter. Bleeding-heart combines well with ferns and other shade plants, and naturalizes nicely in woodland settings. Its finely cut, fernlike foliage also works well with many spring-flowering bulbs.

In hot or arid areas, cut the foliage after the plant flowers because it yellows and becomes ragged. Propagate by dividing in early spring (in mild climates, in spring or fall). Take root cuttings in spring.

CAMPANULA
Also called bellflower
Campanula sp.

Zone: 3

Height: 6 inches to 3 feet

Bloom Time: Early summer

Comments: A mainstay in many perennial gardens, campanula comes in a nearly endless array of growth habits. Species range from low, sprawling types suited for edgings and rock gardens to upright types that produce vertical, spirelike flower stalks.

Plant in full sun (in hot climates, in partial shade) in moist, well-drained soil amended with organic matter. Remove faded flowers to encourage continued blooming. Divide every three or four years, replanting strong divisions from the outer portion of the clump. Strong-

growing types may require division every other year in mild climates. Mulch after the ground freezes in areas where winters are severe. Many types grow easily and quickly from seeds.

CANDYTUFT
Also called iberis
Iberis sempervirens

Zone: 3

Height: 6 to 12 inches

Bloom Time: Late spring

Comments: Candytuft produces a low compact mound of dark green foliage smothered with snow-white flowers in spring. If sheared after flowering, it often reblooms in fall in areas with a long growing season. Because it is low growing, candytuft is ideal for edgings, in rock gardens, as an underplanting with late-flowering tulips, or in combination with other low-growing plants.

Plant in full sun (in hot, arid climates, in partial shade). It does best with regular watering, and in fertile, amended soil. Candytuft is evergreen in mild climates but does not grow well in Gulf Coast areas. In cold climates, it may die back to the ground. Mulch after the ground freezes. Divide in early spring (in mild climates, in fall), or take stem cuttings after the spring growth matures slightly.

CHRYSANTHEMUM
Also called mum or garden mum
Chrysanthemum x morifolium

Zone: 4

Height: 1 to 4 feet

Bloom Time: Fall

Comments: For reliable flowering from late summer to hard frost, and for ease of growth, these plants are hard to beat. Cushion mums produce dense, compact low mounds smothered with flowers. Other types grow to 4 feet. Flowers come in all colors but blue, and in many forms.

Plant in full sun in moist, well-drained soil. Use low-growing types in the front of perennial borders or as an edging elsewhere. Use taller types as cut flowers. All types grow well in containers.

Propagate by stem cuttings or by dividing clumps in spring when new shoots are 2 inches tall. In mild climates, divide yearly. Pinch stem tips to encourage compact growth and lots of flowers. Pinch weekly until mid-July, then stop to let buds form.

COLUMBINE
Aquilegia sp.

Zone: 4

Height:: 15 inches to 2½ feet

Bloom Time: Late spring

Comments: Columbine is a colorful, spring-flowering perennial at home in several garden locations. It's widely used in the middle of perennial gardens, in rock gardens, in wildflower gardens, and mingled among late-flowering tulips. The graceful plants produce arching sprays of white, yellow, pink, red, blue, or bicolored crown-shape flowers. Many types have long spurs projecting backward from the flower.

Plant in full sun in areas with cool summers; otherwise, partial shade. Soil must be well drained. Propagate by sowing seeds in spring or late summer. Only vigorous-growing types produce enough crowns to make division practical.

COREOPSIS
Also called tickseed
Coreopsis sp.

Zone: 4

Height: 8 inches to 2½ feet

Bloom Time: June to frost

Comments: A dependable and easy-to-grow perennial, coreopsis is known for its long flowering season. The golden yellow, daisylike flowers, either single or semidouble, make lovely summer bouquets. Plant in full sun, in well-drained soil. Sow seeds in late summer, or divide plants in early spring every three or four years.

Daylily

DAYLILY
Hemerocallis hybrids

Zone: 3

Height: 1½ to 3½ feet

Bloom Time: Late spring to fall

Comments: Daylilies are reliable, easy to grow, and nearly maintenance free. Although individual flowers usually last only one day, each plant blooms for several weeks. Planting early, mid-season, and late varieties ensures flowers all summer and into fall. Some varieties are repeat bloomers. Daylilies produce clusters of trumpet-shape flowers atop strong stocks. Flowers are available in all colors except blue and pure white; some are bicolored.

Plant in full sun or partial afternoon shade, in moist, well-drained soil. Plant them in gardens according to their heights. Use in the filtered shade of high-branched trees, in sunny spots in woodland gardens, on gentle slopes, or in broad drifts in lawn areas. Short varieties are ideal in containers. Propagate by dividing after flowering is completed in late summer or fall. Vigorous-growing varieties may require dividing every four or five years.

DELPHINIUM
Delphinium sp.

Zone: 4

Height: 2½ to 6 feet

Bloom Time: Early summer; rebloom in fall

Comments: Delphiniums have few rivals for producing a bold display of tall flowers with a strong vertical accent. Most varieties fit best in the back of a perennial garden. Flowers are predominantly blue, but also come in white, pink, and lavender.

Plant in full sun, in moist, well-drained soil. Protect from wind, and provide support as flower stalks develop. Most types rebloom in fall if you cut off the flower stalks just above ground level right after they fade. They also are heavy feeders. In cold climates, mulch after the soil freezes, or overwinter in a cold frame. Propagate from seeds sown in spring or midsummer. Spring-sown dwarf varieties often flower the same year. Divide established clumps in early spring (in mild climates, in fall).

DIANTHUS
Also called pink
Dianthus sp.

Zone: 4

Height: 6 to 15 inches

Bloom Time: Spring and early summer

Comments: The dianthus genus includes several popular perennials grown for their pink, white, or red flowers borne above mats or clumps of grayish-blue, grassy leaves. Most are fragrant; some blend two colors.

Plant in full sun, in well-drained soil amended with organic matter. Most species don't tolerate hot, arid conditions. Some need winter protection with a loose mulch such as evergreen branches. Pinks rot easily, so avoid mulch that packs tightly.

Rejuvenate clumps about every three years by division, replanting only the vigorous outer growth. Or root recently formed stem cuttings in early summer.

FEVERFEW
Chrysanthemum parthenium

Zone: 4

Height: To 2½ feet

Bloom Time: Summer

Comments: Often listed as matricaria in garden catalogs, feverfew produces masses of 1-inch flowers all summer long. Typical flowers are single and daisylike, with white petals and a yellow center. To keep plants blooming and to prevent reseeding, cut off flowers as they fade.

Feverfew is ideal for filling voids in the summer garden, and combines well with most brightly colored flowers. Both its foliage and flowers are scented. Plant in full sun, in nearly any soil. Propagate by dividing in early spring every three or four years, by taking stem cuttings in midsummer, or by sowing seeds.

GERANIUM
Also called cranesbill geranium
Geranium sp.

Zone: 4

Height: 6 inches to 1½ feet

Bloom Time: Spring and summer

Comments: Often confused with the genus pelargonium (also commonly called geranium), cranesbill geranium is a hardy perennial that forms low mounds of color in late spring and summer. Where summers are mild, some species bloom all season long. Flowers are pink, magenta, and purple, with deeply cut, attractive foliage. All are used as edging plants; some are used in rock and wall gardens.

Cranesbill geraniums require no special care. They flower in full sun or partial shade, and do well in poor soil. In fact, soil too fertile causes spindly growth and sparse flowering. Divide eestablished clumps every four or five years in early spring. (In mild climates, divide them in fall.)

HELIANTHUS
Also called perennial sunflower
Helianthus decapetalus 'multiflorus'

Zone: 4

Height: To 6 feet

Bloom Time: Late summer into fall

Comments: Because of its height, helianthus is a perfect choice for the back of a garden or the center of a large island bed. It provides masses of color, usually deep yellow, from late summer to the end of fall. Flowers may be single and daisylike, or double and frilly.

Plant in full sun; otherwise, they develop weak, floppy stems with few flowers. Soil should be well drained. Propagate by dividing every three or four years in spring.

Directory of Perennials

Hosta

HELLEBORUS
Also called Christmas rose
Helleborus niger

or lenten rose
H. orientalis

Zone: 4

Height: 1 to 1½ feet

Bloom Time: Late fall to spring

Comments: Christmas and lenten roses are unusual because they bloom during the winter. Christmas rose can bloom any time from December to April; lenten rose will bloom a little later, usually between March and May. Both plants thrive in a partially shaded location with a rich, woodsy soil. Flowers are borne on slender stalks. Colors include purple, white, pink, and green. Propagate by dividing established clumps in spring after flowering. Lenten rose often reseeds naturally. Move seedlings in spring.

HOSTA
Also called plantain lily or funkia
Hosta sp.

Zone: 4

Height: To 3 feet

Bloom Time: Summer to early fall

Comments: Hostas are among the most useful and decorative perennials for areas of shade to partial shade. They range from 4-inch miniatures to 3-foot giants, and have both attractive foliage and showy flowers. Leaf colors, patterns, and textures include blue, green, variegated, smooth, and quilted. Leaf shapes range from lance to round, in all sizes. Lilylike spiked blooms of white, blue, or pale lavender open in summer.

Hostas are rarely bothered by pests and tolerate many adverse growing conditions. To increase plants, cut and divide. Roots are tough; it's safe to pull them apart.

ICELAND POPPY
Papaver nudicaule

Zone: 5

Height: 12 to 15 inches

Bloom Time: Spring; in mild areas, also in winter

Comments: Few plants rival Iceland poppies for their show of crepe-paperlike flowers up to 4 inches across in a wide array of colors. Most are sold as a color mix and include warm tones such as gold and red along with lighter cream and yellow. Flowers emerge from puffy, drooping buds and are carried on wiry stalks.

These poppies are short-lived perennials and need replanting every few years. Although they originated in arctic areas, they survive and perform best where winters are mild and summers are fairly cool and moist. Start plants using seeds sown in late summer. Provide winter protection in harsh climates. Overwintered plants begin flowering in early spring, and make good companions for spring-flowering bulbs. Where winters are mild, Iceland poppies flower all winter and spring.

IRIS
Iris sp.

Zone: 4 (most species)

Height: 6 to 50 inches

Bloom Time: Spring to early summer

Comments: Easy-to-grow, iris are available in at least six major classifications: tall bearded, dwarf bearded, Dutch, Japanese, Siberian, and spuria. All come in an array of colors, sizes, and varieties. The most commonly grown, the bearded iris, is also one of the most magnificent plants in the perennial garden. Flowers are solids or bicolors, in any color imaginable. Foliage is swordlike. Some are sweetly scented. Plant in full sun with average, well-drained soil. Plant rhizomes in late summer by placing them horizontally with the fan of foliage above the soil. Divide every four years.

JUPITER'S-BEARD
Also called red valerian
Centranthus ruber

Zone: 4

Height: 3 feet

Bloom Time: Spring to early summer

Comments: Perfect for the middle or back of a perennial garden, jupiter's-beard has masses of white, pink, crimson, or red flowers. Blooms are sweet scented and long lasting, making them a good choice for cut-flower arrangements. In mild climates, flowering begins in early spring; otherwise, expect flowers from late spring to early summer. Whether planted in sun or partial shade and regardless of the type of soil, Jupiter's-beard will take off and rarely need attention.

Start new plants by dividing established clumps in early spring or just after flowering. Or dig young seedlings from around mother plants, but expect some color variation. Jupiter's-beard self-sows, and may need controlling to keep it from taking over the garden.

LUPINE
Lupinus sp.

Zone: 4

Height: 3 to 4 feet

Bloom Time: Spring through summer, if cool

Comments: Although native varieties of lupine are numerous, the only strain lending itself to use in most home gardens is a group called Russell hybrids. They are commonly available in blue, pink, red, yellow, purple, and bicolors. Foliage is deeply cut and attractive.

Because of their tall, stately appearance, they are best planted as a mass in back-of-the-border locations. In windy areas, some staking might be necessary. Lupines thrive in cool weather. You can start them from seeds, but they will not bloom for at least two years. It is best to buy transplants for early spring planting.

ORIENTAL POPPY
Papaver orientale

Zone: 3

Height: 2 to 4 feet

Bloom Time: Late spring to early summer

Comments: Oriental poppies supply breathtaking, flamboyant color to spring and early summer gardens. Colors include white, pink, orange, and various shades of red, each with a dark contrasting center. Flowers open from large, nodding buds atop stems carried well above the gray-green foliage. Blooms may be as large at 6 inches.

Foliage is coarse and hairy; stems grow 2 to 4 feet tall. Poppies like average, well-drained soil. The foliage disappears after the plants bloom, then reappears in early fall, so fill in with annuals to avoid bare spots all summer.

PEONY
Paeonia sp.

Zone: 3

Height: 2 to 4 feet

Bloom Time: Late spring to early summer

Comments: Peonies are legendary for their colorfully showy flowers, their reliability, and their easy care. Flowers are mostly white, pink, maroon, or red, and are favorites for cutting. They may be single, semidouble, double, or a special form. All have a delicious scent. Use in mixed perennial gardens, in front of hedges and evergreen plantings, in large drifts in lawn areas, bordering walks and driveways, along fences and walls, and as specimens. Use them in cut arrangements as well.

Peonies die to the ground in winter, producing spring growth up to 4 feet tall. Install stakes or peony ring supports early to avoid damage from wind and rain. Plant peonies in full sun or light shade and in rich, moist, well-drained soil. Mulch in both summer and winter. Propagate by dividing them every six to 10 years.

PHLOX
Phlox sp.

Zone: 3

Height: To 4 feet

Bloom Time: Spring, summer, or early fall

Comments: An old favorite, phlox varieties offer spring-blooming dwarf plants ideal for rock gardens and stately summer plants up to 4 feet tall. Colors include white, red, pink, blue, and lavender. Many have a contrasting center.

Plant in full sun or partial shade, and in moist, well-drained soil. Propagate by sowing seeds in midsummer, by dividing established clumps just after flowering, or by taking firm, leafy stem cuttings in the summer.

POKER PLANT
Also called torch lily or red hot poker
Kniphofia sp.

Zone: 5

Height: 3 to 5 feet

Bloom Time: Midsummer through fall

Poker plant

Comments: Known for its tall, impressive flower spikes, often with a vivid blend of scarlet and yellow blooms, poker plant also is offered as a hybrid in white, yellow, orange, and scarlet. The clumps of grassy, gray-green leaves grow 3 feet tall. Flowers attract hummingbirds and are suitable for arrangements.

Use singly as specimens or in small groupings at the back of a border. Plant in full sun, but protect them from heavy winds. Soil should be sandy and well drained. Propagate by dividing established clumps in spring in cold climates and in spring or fall in mild climates.

PRIMROSE
Primula sp.

Zone: 3 to 5 (depending on variety)

Height: To 15 inches

Bloom Time: Early spring

Comments: Primroses form one of the largest families of popular garden plants. Virtually every flower color but green is available, and many are bicolored with frilled or sculpted petal edges.

Plant in partial shade in rich, moist soil. Some types grow well in boggy locations. Propagate by sowing seeds in midsummer. Protect seedlings in harsh-winter climates. In mild climates, divide in early autumn.

RUDBECKIA
Also called black-eyed susan
Rudbeckia sp.

Zone: 4

Height: To 3 feet

Bloom Time: Summer through fall

Comments: Rudbeckias produce masses of golden yellow, daisylike flowers with contrasting centers from midsummer until frost. Plants are rugged and easy to grow, and provide superb cut flowers. They are ideally suited to the middle portion of a sunny perennial garden, and tolerate nearly any soil type, as long as it is well drained.

Directory of Perennials

Soggy soil, especially in winter, causes crown rot. Drought tolerant, rudbeckia can be propagated by seed or division. Where the growing season is short, sow seeds in midsummer for flowering the following year.

SALVIA
Also called sage
Salvia sp.

Zone: 4

Height: 2 to 5 feet

Bloom Time: Summer to fall

Comments: Often considered an annual flower, salvia has several perennial varieties, including the type used as a cooking herb and types grown for their showy flowers—mostly blue or violet. Salvia is a good plant for mid- or back-of-the-border locations.

Plant in full sun or partial afternoon shade in almost any well-drained soil. Propagate by division or stem cuttings. Seeds of some types are available and grow easily.

SEDUM
Also called stonecrop
Sedum sp.

Zone: 3

Height: 4 inches to 2 feet

Bloom Time: Spring to late summer

Comments: Commonly used in rock or wall gardens, many sedums also make first-rate ground covers and edging plants in perennial gardens. Most also are perfectly suited to containers. Sedum flowers are small but are borne in large, showy clusters of red, pink, cream, white, yellow, or rust. Bees and butterflies flock to them.

All sedums are fleshy leaved and quite drought tolerant. Plant in full sun or partial shade in well-drained soil. Propagate by dividing or by taking stem or leaf cuttings. Seeds are available for some types.

VERONICA
Also called speedwell
Veronica sp.

Zone: 4

Height: 6 inches to 3 feet

Bloom Time: June to September

Comments: The veronica genus has several species in a range of sizes, some suitable for use in rock gardens, as ground covers, or as low edgings, and others for use in mid- to back-of-the-garden locations. Most have blue, spikelike flowers, but pink and white forms are available.

Plant veronica in a sunny, well-drained location. The plant grows well in heat and is fairly drought tolerant. Divide established clumps after flowering but before mid-autumn. Divide every four or five years to keep plants vigorous.

YARROW
Achillea sp.

Zone: 3

Height: 8 inches to 5 feet

Bloom Time: June to September

Comments: Yarrow is known for its ferny foliage and showy flat flowers, its ease of growth, and its range of heights. Flowers may be white, yellow, or pink, or shades in between. Heights range from the 8-inch woolly yarrow, a ground cover, to the 5-foot fern-leaf yarrow.

Plant in full sun because even a small amount of shade reduces flowering and makes tall plants floppy. Yarrow tolerates rugged conditions, and average soil is suitable as long as it is well drained. Propagate by dividing in spring or in early fall after flowering.

Zone Map

Consider Your Climate The key to successful gardening is knowing what plants are best suited to your area and when to plant them. This is true for every type of gardening. Climate maps, such as the one opposite, give a good idea of the extremes in temperature by zones. The zone-number listings tell you the coldest temperature a plant typically can edure.

By choosing plants best adapted to the different zones, and by planting them at the right time, you will have many more successes.

The climate in your area is a mixture of many different weather patterns: sun, snow, rain, wind, and humidity. To be a good gardener, you should know, on an average, how cold the garden gets in winter, how much rainfall it receives each year, and how hot or dry it becomes in a typical summer. You can obtain this general information from your state agricultural school or your county extension agent. In addition, acquaint yourself with the mini-climates in your neighborhood, based on such factors as wind protection gained from a nearby hill, or humidity and cooling offered by a local lake or river. Then carry the research further by studying the microclimates that characterize your own plot of ground.

Here are a few points to keep in mind:

■ Plants react to exposure. Southern and western exposures are sunnier and warmer than northern or eastern ones. Light conditions vary greatly even in a small yard. Match your plants' needs to the correct exposure.

■ Wind can damage many plants, by either drying the soil or knocking over fragile growth. Protect plants from both summer and winter winds to increase their odds of survival and to save yourself the time and energy of staking plants and watering more frequently.

■ Consider elevation, too, when selecting plants. Cold air sweeps down hills and rests in low areas. These frost pockets are fine for some plantings, deadly for others. Plant vegetation that prefers a warmer environment on the tops or sides of hills, never at the bottom.

■ Use fences, the sides of buildings, shrubs, and trees to your advantage. Watch the play of shadows, the sweep of winds, and the flow of snowdrifts in winter. These varying situations are ideal for some plants, harmful to others. In short, always look for ways to make the most of everything your yard has to offer.

THE USDA PLANT HARDINESS MAP
OF THE UNITED STATES AND CANADA

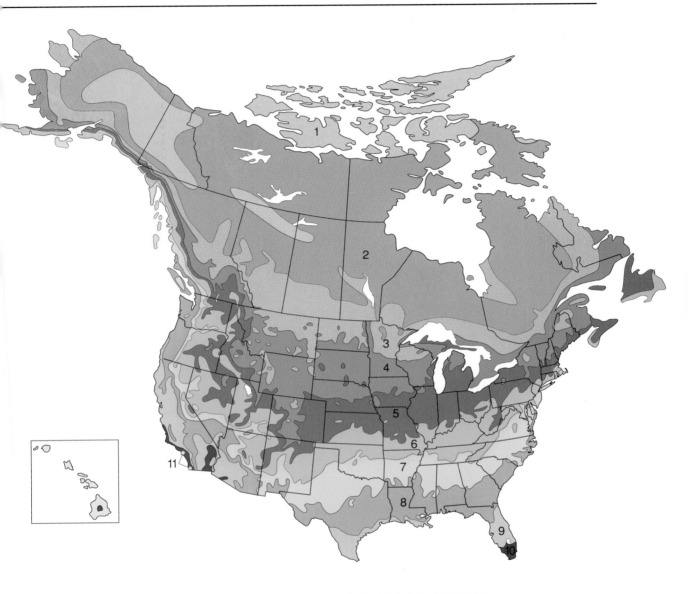

RANGE OF AVERAGE ANNUAL MINIMUM
TEMPERATURES FOR EACH ZONE

	ZONE 1	BELOW -50° F
	ZONE 2	-50° TO -40°
	ZONE 3	-40° TO -30°
	ZONE 4	-30° TO -20°
	ZONE 5	-20° TO -10°
	ZONE 6	-10° TO 0°
	ZONE 7	0° TO 10°
	ZONE 8	10° TO 20°
	ZONE 9	20° TO 30°
	ZONE 10	30° TO 40°
	ZONE 11	ABOVE 40°

Index